MW01284563

STAY DEAD

COPPER
CANYON
PRESS

Also by Natalie Shapero

Popular Longing
Hard Child
No Object

STAY DEAD NATALIE SHAPERO

Copper Canyon Press
Port Townsend, Washington

Copyright 2025 by Natalie Shapero
All rights reserved
Printed in the United States of America

Cover art: Golden Vibes Photo, *Desert Disco Vibes,* detail, 2022

Copper Canyon Press is in residence at Fort Worden State Park
in Port Townsend, Washington, under the auspices of Centrum.
Centrum is a gathering place for artists and creative thinkers from
around the world, students of all ages and backgrounds, and
audiences seeking extraordinary cultural enrichment.

LIBRARY OF CONGRESS CATALOGING-IN-PUBLICATION DATA
Names: Shapero, Natalie, author.
Title: Stay dead / Natalie Shapero.
Description: Port Townsend, Washington : Copper Canyon Press, 2025. |
    Summary: "A collection of poems by Natalie Shapero"— Provided by
    publisher.
Identifiers: LCCN 2025010395 (print) | LCCN 2025010396 (ebook) |
    ISBN 9781556597121 (paperback) | ISBN 9781619323216 (epub)
Subjects: LCGFT: Poetry.
Classification: LCC PS3619.H35575 S73 2025 (print) |
    LCC PS3619.H35575 (ebook) | DDC 811/.6—dc23/eng/20250512
LC record available at https://lccn.loc.gov/2025010395
LC ebook record available at https://lccn.loc.gov/2025010396

9 8 7 6 5 4 3 2 FIRST PRINTING

COPPER CANYON PRESS
Post Office Box 271
Port Townsend, Washington 98368
www.coppercanyonpress.org

For you, Ricky—

Contents

Spacewalk　3

Centimeter Ruler　7

Finally, Some Concrete Career Advice　8

Oh Boo Hoo　9

Larger Papers　10

Play In　11

In Something　12

Wrong Line　13

Black on Dark Sienna on Purple　14

Long Week Talking　15

Kilowatt-Hour　16

Fireball　17

No Comets Seen　18

Capacity Crowd　19

Great Scaffold　20

Nightstand　22

Fox　25

True Apothecary　26

Red Item　27

Big Mistake. Big. Huge.　28

Slip　29

How'd You Get This Number　30

Bad Weather, Pourville　31

Push Down and Turn　32

Start   33

Quick Thinking   34

And Shove It   35

First of February   36

Big Basin   37

First of June   38

Here and Only Here   41

Lithol Red   42

Owner Surrender   43

Enough   44

86   45

Suddenly   47

Suffrutescent Scrub   48

I Tune My Body and My Brain to the Music of the Land   49

My Teacher Again   50

Quick Love Note   51

And Certainly Not Least   52

Isolette   53

Remember My Decision for One Day   54

Individual Normal Hill   57

Straight Sets   58

Really Raining   59

Can Art Be Taught   60

No One Calls It That   61

Months At Once   62

Rough Stuff   63

Careful   64

That Endless Skyway   65

First of December   66

Sorry to Eat   67

Have You Been Wanting to Go to Sleep and Not Wake Up   68

Notes   71

Acknowledgments   77

About the Author   79

STAY DEAD

Spacewalk

Big deal, the solar system
is replete with rubble left over from its formation.
Join the club.
All my circulating garbage and nowhere
for it to go. I used to talk stuff out
with the dead, but now I can't even
do that anymore. They stopped understanding
my references. They failed
to intuit tone. We are witnessing an age
of unprecedented divide
between this life and after; they only
want to be with their own.
I'd drown myself, but unfortunately
I can't find the ocean, though it seems like just
a minute ago it was right here,
with its bread-knife fish and its
putty-knife fish and all its landed modules,
down from space.
Travelers, welcome home. I heard
they give each astronaut a pill
to end it all up there if needed. If the spacewalk
turns out bleakest.
Look around. You know what I want
to know. Do they get to keep it.

I DON'T HAVE ANY SEINE RIVER LIKE MONET . . .

(Ed Ruscha)

Centimeter Ruler

I wanted to stop getting high but you know
what they say no sobriety
in the first year of a big life change I think I'm recalling
that right I think I remember

actually everything the movie quote BROTHER
IF YOU CAN'T PAINT IN PARIS, YOU'D BETTER GIVE UP
AND MARRY THE BOSS'S DAUGHTER I thought of it

when my actual boss in not Paris expressed
annoyance at how her godson disavowed
on principle low-wage work but wasn't too good to cash
the checks she sent PERHAPS HE BELIEVES

IN REDISTRIBUTION WITHOUT EXPLOITATION
I did not say because I was being at the time paid
to not say sentences like that but instead
to absorb can someone wring me

out or do I as they say about WANTING SOMETHING
DONE RIGHT have to do it myself

Finally, Some Concrete Career Advice

Don't be an actor. God observes you
violent in a scene and, thinking it is real, mistakenly
adds you to Hell. This happens all the time.
It's like when I traveled
across eight states in shattering
pain to curl beside L as she left this Earth, only to later
have a dream I'd instead stayed home
eating fruit cups and sewing a patch on my jeans.
I didn't know a dream
could undo a true event, uncement it,
but it did—from then on, I hadn't gone, and how
do I live with myself now, I ask each day—

Oh Boo Hoo

Five years on a research study
to unearth why former conscripts wouldn't
talk about the war. It turned out
to be because nobody wanted to hear it.

Have I told you I like your flashlight?
Your trusty one gallon
of water per person per day on the bottom shelf?
It's honestly cute that you think

you know what's coming. Have I told you
about when I died and came back
and everyone begged me
to please stay dead? It wasn't, they promised me, personal—

they'd just gone all out on the funeral, and they didn't
want all that money to be for nothing—

Larger Papers

I've seen enough films where a character nicks
himself shaving or maybe has a bread knife slip and the thin
run of blood is supposed to stand for some violence,
for something he did and is desperate
to cover up, but the truth will out—I've seen enough

that when I graze my own hand on the jag
in the railing and find I've been cut, I ask what did
that symbolize, as though I'm some puny
reporter hollering out at a sought director who is ducking
into a limo—OVER HERE! WHAT DID THE BLOOD
SYMBOLIZE??—and I never

get an answer, I have to read it
in other papers, larger papers, studios taking out
full-page ads so of course they get privileged access, I'm so
resentful that I look away when I see them being
read on benches and beaches, all those sections, business
style metro nation real estate world my god does it ever end

Play In

Often I have been told I should be in movies,
not because I am glamorous or anything like that, but because
my expressions are at times borderline
imperceptible; seeing me from a regular distance, people can't tell
how I feel. So really what they're recommending
is enlargement, the ability to be transmitted to others by close-up.
Isn't there a way to get this accomplished
without becoming an actor? Can't someone wait
until right when the light's good, then hold above me
a magnifying glass, like a cruel child intent on burning a bug?
My hang-up with movies is the messaging

that comes with being filmed out of sequence. It makes actors
confused—they start thinking that in life
they can go ahead and die and then just be fine the next day.
Also sometimes you only get a slice
of the script if you're assigned to a lesser part; you can be in the thing
and not even know what the plot is. Well, I get enough
of that in my own life already. Sometimes I'm sore
from living embargoed, nobody telling me how I play in, but I know
I should just be thankful for the paycheck. I'M LUCKY, I say,
regular sized and largely unreadable, TO BE HERE AT ALL.

In Something

Acting does have its pull. Who doesn't want to be
in something? I PAINT VERY LARGE PICTURES. . . .

TO PAINT A SMALL PICTURE IS TO PLACE YOURSELF
OUTSIDE YOUR EXPERIENCE, TO LOOK UPON AN EXPERIENCE
AS A STEREOPTICON VIEW OR WITH A REDUCING GLASS.
HOWEVER YOU PAINT THE LARGER PICTURE,
YOU ARE IN IT (Rothko).

I've wanted to be in something. I've been terrified
of the converse. To anyone who would listen, I've recited
the sequence of conditions that gave rise to the SoHo Loft:
the industries' exit, the artists squatting
in the hollowed-out factories, how the sheer size
of the spaces allowed for the production of larger and larger works.
How this shifted the vogue—

salon-style decor giving way to the ONE-PICTURE WALL,
the collectors clamoring not only for paintings of increasing
dimension, but also for the loft layouts that were ideal
for their display. The buildings acquired and sold,
the artists priced out. A cautionary tale about painting
oneself right out of one's own life.

Rothko told the story of summer at home
with the windows pushed up, overhearing one passerby
to another I WONDER WHO LIVES IN THIS HOUSE
WITH ALL THE ROTHKOS?

Wrong Line

So badly I've wanted to be IN SOMETHING and now it turns out
I am. What I'm in is the wrong line, the absolute wrong line
of work. Should've been an actor! Though I know what people
are thinking: if acting appeals as a route to rejecting
oneself and becoming instead someone else,
and if I'm unequipped,
                     as I've been in these times, to recognize just
who I am, isn't there a real risk I'll inadvertently step into someone
I do not realize is me? No further questions. So far as I've seen,

the main task of acting is, out of desperation, professing expertise
in whatever is required of the role: OF COURSE
I SPEAK FLEMISH. OF COURSE I CAN POLE-VAULT.
OF COURSE I CAN HIT A HIGH G.
                        OF COURSE I'M A PAINTER, and the next
thing I know, they're plunking me down in front of an easel, watching
in exasperation as I blend carmine and crimson
not on the palette, but straight on my upturned arm, requiring
hospitalization for turpentine poisoning. When the doctor accuses me
of trying to die, I explain it was just for a role. OF COURSE
I CAN SKEET SHOOT. OF COURSE I CAN
HANG GLIDE. OF COURSE I CAN LIVE THROUGH THE YEAR.

Black on Dark Sienna on Purple

I do enjoy beholding the rectilinear pictorial output
of abstract expressionist Markus Yakovlevich Rothkowicz
at the Museum of Contemporary Art in downtown
Los Angeles where the wall text provides not only the artists' places
of birth but also their places of death Giacometti

in Switzerland Arakawa in Manhattan we play a game
where we try to guess how everyone died based on where
they died Chris Burden in Topanga Canyon whenever you die
in a canyon in Southern California it kind of sounds
like you got murdered but maybe die anywhere

and it always kind of sounds like you got murdered even
or especially a studio on East 69th Street the artist
Hedda Sterne born Hedwig Lindenberg in 1910
responded to the news of Rothko's death WHO WAS
THIS MAN, MARK ROTHKO, WHO KILLED MY FRIEND?

Long Week Talking

I am ashamed to keep thinking of death
as a chute that connects to the garbage. I know I should
picture it more like the pneumatic tubes
at banks of the past: you put in your name and your paper and up
you go. I know a bank

should be the operative metaphor
for every facet of existence, every time.
When I fail to liken anything to a bank, I must be tired.
That's not the real me; that's the long week talking. Time

for bed. Time for the open window and my head
on the narrow pillow. The hectoring sky. The streetlight's
beam is bright as the bright saved people
see when they die, but I don't die—

Kilowatt-Hour

I didn't pin it as grief at first, the feeling
of imagining placing myself
in the path of that truck, but of course
it was grief, grief for myself
in the future—not being around
down the road to feel it, I had to start
feeling it now, I had to make sure

I would not leave the world with my feelings
unfinished, that everything needing
to be sensed would have been
fully sensed, and by me, the way that T
in her old age explained
that she always paid off the electric bill
promptly so as to save

her dear ones the trouble of running
around in her absence ascertaining
what was owed and to whom—I could
have responded that zero and zero
only is owed to any extractive
conglomeration, but she had no moment
to hear this, nor to hear

anything—she was too busy
dying, too busy working
to leave the world, the world like a blur
of chassis and axle, the world
like a lace-white twenty-six-foot moving
truck she was dodging, jumping
to safety just in time—

Fireball

Please stop circulating the untrue rumor
that I have been telling people I hope there is
no Heaven, that one world
is enough. Bandages stocked
in the padlocked aisle, claim denial, bird
spikes, rent hikes, people sleeping in arrays
of rags and being categorized as rags—why
wouldn't I want more of what God made?

You said NATURE IS INDIFFERENT
TO SUFFERING. I said whoa you and nature
have so much in common—you should get
together sometime. Listen, if it looks like
I'm dying, I'm not—I'm just burning
up in Earth's atmosphere like comet debris
on impact, piercing the field
and then flashing away. It should be any day.

No Comets Seen

Watching somebody squash a bug, I'm screaming
YOU'LL NEVER KILL US ALL, and, yeah,
I realize I'm not an insect—it's just that we have so much
in common: we both sometimes eat chunks of poison; we both
do not subscribe to Hell; we both have never read JULIUS CAESAR,
though I at least have a decent sense
of both the noonday stabbing and Calpurnia's premonition.
I can't believe my old neighbor was right

when he told me that either robots or royals
would have our jobs by end of quarter four. He should take that
skill on tour. I've tried to know the future,
but my specialty's really the past. I've been living
for the bugs who've died, to remember them; it's a good
bet some other bug will be living soon for me.

Capacity Crowd

I'm sick of waiting for this city to work
me out of itself like a splinter. I'm sick
of producing my own subsistence
as a way to literally express my being alive.
I'm sorry to have died and not really
noticed, but I've been so busy loving
what you're wearing and pouring
my paint right into the dip in the street
that drains to the sea. I never saw myself
represented in art until that movie
where the one guy is fed to the wood-
chipper: bye! I was so proud I cried.

Great Scaffold

In Boston, they don't call it SUMMER. They call it CONSTRUCTION SEASON.
Birds sing all night, I was told, because in the day they can no longer
make themselves heard over the pickup and drop-off of various slabs.

I was trying to list the six principal pollutants.
I was trying to remember a line by Blaise Cendrars.

The middle part escaped me. PARIS / CITY OF THE ONLY TOWER
AND THE SOMETHING ELSE AND THE WHEEL.

I visited a home I was wanting to rent. The landlord explained she had gotten
a deal by purchasing the place in the close aftermath
of a highly publicized rape in a nearby park.

I relayed this information to L. He shrugged and said BOSTON.

That was the thing about Boston. Whatever you tried to tell someone,
they would simply shrug and say back to you BOSTON.

I said I once woke here in stratospheric fever, and I went to the immediate
hospital, which had recently been in the news for poor
lighting and signage. Someone died on the concrete
outside, unsure how to get in.

He shrugged and said BOSTON.

And I said I keep trying to watch TV, but the way they cut together
the salient previous points of the plot, to catch up the casual viewer—
it makes me think of reconstructing
a heinous event through a haze of drugs. The splintered
recollecting, flash by flash.

He shrugged and said BOSTON.

And I said I know people who've floated themselves
away from their bodies in times of wounding, but I didn't do that. I was
in there. I was in there. It was only later, on an unchosen day and with
no gesture of warning, that I exited and could not
get back in. And I have lived since beside myself, and I am afraid
I will die here, struggling around for some unfindable door.

He shrugged and said BOSTON.

BOSTON / CITY OF THE BIRDSONG
AND THE SOMETHING ELSE AND THE WHEEEEEEEEEEEEEEEEEEEEL

Nightstand

I keep picking up the book about trauma and recovery, but right
when I get to the end of section one, the door rings, the dog pukes,
the heater blows, fraud alert, tornado drill, get out
here fast, you gotta see this truck that ignored the height sign
on the underpass and now it's lodged like an overlarge pill
in the throat of the off-ramp, tangling the city where I poison
myself with the past, cough it up, cough it up—

I FIND MYSELF DISGUSTED BY MY PROFESSION . . .

(Claude Monet)

Fox

I tried the pills. They didn't help me sleep,
but that was no big deal. I'LL SLEEP WHEN I'M DEAD. And they also
didn't bring relief, but what can you do. I'LL BE RELIEVED
WHEN I'M DEAD. I stayed in bed
or sunned in the drive like some kind of studio
head's side piece. I got into watching these clips
where women online showcased the clothes they wore
or the food they ate on a given day. The best account was the one
where the videos often concluded with OBVIOUSLY.
AND I PAIRED THIS WITH MY ROUND RATTAN CROSS-BODY BAG, OBVIOUSLY.
FOR DESSERT, I HAD TWO PEACHES. OBVIOUSLY. I needed,
I decided, a fur coat. Everyone was surprised. It didn't
seem like me. But I was trying whatever I could,
in case it kept me from dying. I was trying
not to die. I'LL DIE WHEN I'M DEAD. The coat was from the '60s
and unmaintained. It cost me forty-five dollars plus shipping and tax.
I wore it a lot. The fur was falling off.
I rented a car and drove in the coat and then received a bill
for disobeying the rule against pets in the car.
The bill was two hundred dollars. The fur was everywhere. The coat
was from the '60s and it cost me forty-five dollars plus two hundred dollars
plus shipping and tax. And it might have kept me
from dying, in which case it cost me forty-five dollars
plus two hundred dollars plus shipping and tax plus rent plus food plus internet
plus gas plus etc. times twelve and then times however many
more years I would end up alive. The most expensive coat in history.
Sometimes people asked me what it was. I didn't even
begin to know how to know. Rabbits got killed for coats. Also chinchillas.
It could have been a fox. It could have been a mink coat, obviously.

True Apothecary

Having been a kid amid the release and reception
of the Alanis Morissette song IRONIC, having absorbed the scoffing
over how some scenarios detailed within
were not in fact IRONIC—this made me shy,

going forward, to term things IRONIC, in case I was getting it wrong—
I even hesitated to attach the label to Romeo
ending his life a mere half hour prior to Juliet waking,
though of course that's ironic—

each next day is just getting berated or scraping
against what the state won't fix or aching at the door, and still
I wept when you said that to be here is sacred—I wept in agreement—

and also I wept because each next day is Juliet waking, yet taking her
for dead when she looks so dead—a mistake who wouldn't be
forgiven for making—

Red Item

I don't smoke. I know it's dangerous, I say now
of the sun instead, but I shun the advice to avoid it.
I just have to have it right on me. I feel bad

for the people in the movie where the ovular vessels
from outer space cause a shadow
over all of Los Angeles. It's not the sun

we need less of. It's the moon. Less of its blankness.
Less of its compliance. Its wholesomeness.
Its spotless beam. Like a work shirt. I feel bad

for the laundromat in the movie where one red item
is washed with a load of lights. It's bad
to have that in you. The moment when everything's ruined.

Big Mistake. Big. Huge.

Mark Rothko was just too trusting
when he announced I'M INTERESTED ONLY
IN EXPRESSING BASIC HUMAN
EMOTIONS—TRAGEDY, ECSTACY, DOOM,
AND SO ON. Personally, I couldn't begin
to fill in what the other ones are.
Is one of them the feeling of overly
enjoying the joke WHAT'S BLUE
AND SMELLS LIKE RED PAINT
(BLUE PAINT)? Is one of them not
being able to remember
which director it was who said,
regarding violence in his movies, THAT'S NOT
BLOOD; THAT'S RED? Is one of them
returning from the dead? Strolling
back into the world, I felt like the movies:
Julia Roberts in PRETTY WOMAN,
decked out and making her beeline
for the boutique that declined to serve her:
BIG MISTAKE. BIG. HUGE. The mulberry
silk. The gold brocade. Is one
of them they could've had it made.

Slip

I did try to kill, I have caught myself
saying to friends, the man who killed me. I somehow keep

forgetting he didn't complete it. I have no mind
for details. My life—it's like a movie

I view on an airplane. A distraction.
I'm at best half-sure what happened. I want to start
over. The wail when they lower

the high-grade aluminum wheels at 165 miles per hour—
a powerful part. I hit the ground hard.

How'd You Get This Number

I couldn't stomach a movie about it, after
it happened to me—that's why I make lists
of plausible additional upcoming shocks,
then scramble to watch all films on these subjects
while I still find them fun. You remember the one
with the woman walking forever in winter?
Everyone loves that actor, but they found the plotting
shoddy and too spare. They said she was
wasted on that role. Like you were wasted

on this world—I'm the real one who belongs here,
who suits its din and disuse.
After you'd gone, I prayed for myself
to outdo my prior low era, so that I could feel
solace at the thought of how you never
lived to see it. I tithed, I ignited
a votive. I did not have to wait long.

Bad Weather, Pourville

What did we do to the ocean to make it
hurl itself on the rocks like that,
no one to jump in after it—

   Water fills me with horror.
PAINTING FILLS ME WITH HORROR

AS WATER DOES A RABID
DOG (Claude Monet). I feel awful

   about comparing myself
  to the ocean. I don't have nearly

that much plastic in me. I can't presume
to imagine what that's like. I DON'T HAVE

ANY SEINE RIVER LIKE MONET. I'VE JUST GOT
the liminal space

   between this world
  and the next. This world fills me

with horror, how the water hits the light. WHAT
DID ONE CANDLE SAY TO THE OTHER?
LET'S GO

  OUT TONIGHT.

Push Down and Turn

The practice of acting is often described as PRIVACY
IN PUBLIC, which historically has at times been conflated
with SECRECY, inviting suspicion and scorn. I admit
I have trouble telling the one from the other. Is it PRIVACY
or SECRECY to have never revealed to anyone
that living through this has been like shaking awake

during surgery—I'm down here trying to feel my own
shock, but I can't feel anything except their terror
at their own neglect and their desperation
to know will I even remember, and, if I remember, will I forgive—

Start

I don't like how the second you don't die

you're a survivor—there should be some between
period where you don't have to be that quite
yet, like how when needlegrass gets torn out

by the roots, the life within it
doesn't beam straight into some other shoot;

there's a minute or river of minutes—everyone needs
to slow down, debrief, no new
sobriquet at this time, please—the only speed

I want in my life is to sleep and then wake

with a start, the way they do
in representations of dreaming on film, not wake
as I do now, lightly from the nightmare,

head raw and a haze of being unsure
if it all was real, which means it was.

Quick Thinking

I mean it. I don't want to be called a SURVIVOR.
I don't want to be called a SURVIVOR so much that I just went ahead
and died: problem solved. That's called
QUICK THINKING. That's called WOMEN'S INGENUITY.
Everyone wants to know if I now miss the world
or at least its insensate components, such as the pulling apart
of Parker House Rolls or the clarity that comes
with knowing that pull-apart Parker House Rolls
are named for the Omni Parker House, formerly the Parker House
located on School Street in Boston and notable for briefly
employing in the kitchen both Ho Chi Minh
and Malcolm X, who share—and now we're getting to the part
of the world that I do miss—a May 19 birthday. I love
a good fact. I love how Mark Rothko's brothers
truncated ROTHKOWITZ to ROTH, while he went weirder.
I love how NO. 1 (ROYAL RED AND BLUE) exceeded by forty million dollars
its presale estimate of thirty-five. I love knowing
that death is less like a choice and more
like being sucked out of the open door of an airplane. Is it selfish
to be sucked out of the open door of an airplane? Is it weak
to dignify the world, a world no longer mine? Its markets
and its solvents and its tyrants always talking
about how they're redoing their windows, how they're shifting
to extruded aluminum with the rot-resistant
cladding? I WOULD LOVE TO KNOW MORE
ABOUT THAT, I purred. Love was of course the wrong word.

And Shove It

Each year on Earth is like a day
at the ice rink, freezing and slumping
in the stands while the skaters
cruise by and I'm watching them
circle and circle like I'm some
astronaut drifting in wait of descent,
tabulating blandly, patched
through to the planet and fielding
complaints and blanching
down through the pressure panes
of tempered silica glass Hey take this job—

First of February

One hassle after another You said you must
have done something cruel
in a former life to deserve all this Well hon I'm here

to bring you the news it was actually
this life Yes the one right now
Yes I can pinpoint like eight times you flashed

a grin at suffering subordinates and then zipped
to the personal trainer Or don't
you remember Well we all

get I guess turned around Take me
I bought it when they said
I'll get reunited in death with my dead I went

to school I worked for tips The world it saw me
coming It licked its lips

Big Basin

Five hours and forty-three minutes to get to the redwood,
at which point a voice announced from the sky
ONE OF YOU DOWN THERE IS NINE HUNDRED YEARS OLD—

it didn't specify which of us, but I'm pretty sure
it meant me—

I'm just so degraded. I couldn't have gotten this degraded
in a few decades' time.

When I let out my dog in the sage scrub,
to deter the coyotes I'm yelling A PERSON'S HERE, TOO—
but in truth I don't know if I am
a person, or if I'm just an anthropomorphic iteration
of the knowledge that the idiom CUT TO THE CHASE
originated in film editing; it's just what you do

when your action movie borders on the overlong—

I've bordered on the overlong. I've sustained
an unregenerate burn. I've died and, out of boredom,
returned. I've thrown a stone

down the well of myself, listening for the smack
against the clay bottom. I never heard it. I went on forever—

First of June

I keep getting older
which I'm not entirely sure is a good idea

as everyone knows that in afterlife you stay
the age at which you died

I keep repeating
in my head I MISSED MY CHANCE

I MISSED MY CHANCE to be this
age or that one forever

the grain unstacks
the Seine goes red the garden's overgrown

everything changes except
I guess for stone

. . . EVERYTHING CHANGES, EVEN STONE

(Claude Monet)

Here and Only Here

You know what they say: TODAY HAMLET,
TOMORROW A SUPERNUMERARY. You know
what they say: today planet Earth, tomorrow
consignment to Hell. I've had enough

with these people who feel so superior
to the dead all the time. Who flaunt their beats
and pulses. Who ostentatiously obsess
over things only living people know of,

the origin of the word ENDEMIC
or the overrepresentation, in movies and TV,
of one red item going through
the wash with a load of lights. Though, trust me,

it does happen. It happens more than you think.
Weddings, blessings, laboratories.
Fencing, tennis, hotel kitchens.
Painters on their scaffold towers. Pink.

Lithol Red

Truly, it is not good to be an actor. It is better
to be a painter, to be something
with the potential to have one's work degraded by the sun.
To really fear it. I practice at home
with fruit. I set them on the sill for weeks
and observe them turning sallow. Worst is the tomato.
I see myself in its red. It demands
its own kind of knife. It's so prissy. Just for once get cut,
why don't you, with what cuts everyone else—

Owner Surrender

I was low. I told him he should give me his blessing
to die and he said YOU CAN HAVE IT
WHEN YOU'RE NINETY. Baby, don't
tease. Baby, how can you
be sure I'm not ninety now? Have you even considered
I might be like one of those dogs where the shelter plays
fast and loose with the age? You think
you've got a two-year-old, but he's seven.
You think you're dealing with a pup, but she's fifteen.
Baby, would you rather have a runaway or one
that got tested out and then returned?
OWNER SURRENDER, they call it. Even then, you can't
be sure; you can only try—assess
the incisor, examine the eye, measure
the buildup, track the milky haze—but the fact
is that, with a typical dog, there is no way to precisely
clock the age. You just have to wait, unknowing,
for some next phase. Baby, can you tell
if I'm different? Am I changing? Will I change?

Enough

Really lately I haven't been speaking well. Saying I CARTED MY BELONGINGS
INTO THE DUMPSTER, when everyone knows that the verb TO CART
suggests or even demands the direct involvement of a wheeled conveyance,
and I used only my body. Believe me, buddy, the last thing I want

is to take advantage of your trust in me to misrepresent myself as vehicular.
And I especially want to not say I CARTED MY BELONGINGS
INTO THE DUMPSTER AFTER HE TRIED TO TAKE MY LIFE,
which makes it sound as though MY LIFE is something only one person
may possess at a given time. There's enough,
in the same way they used to say about love, to go around. Whoever

wants it is welcome to the part where I read all about how Monet
developed a system of lowering a massive canvas into a trench in order
to paint the top. Whoever wants to can think how I personally probably
would've instead used the floor and a ladder, but, hey, to each their own.
And don't hesitate to help yourself to the feeling of having once been stoked

to not be a painter, to not put my work into singular objects
that must be then relinquished and hung God-knows-where. Don't
hesitate to feel how, as it turned out, I would give essentially
anything to once and forever just get all these words the fuck away from me.

Regarding suicide and its behaviors, two lines that again and again
come to mind are I ROCKED SHUT // AS A SEASHELL (Sylvia Plath)
and IT SLAMMED ME SHUT LIKE A BOOK (Anthony Bourdain), except
Bourdain wasn't writing about self-harm, his subject there was a SINGLE
BAD MUSSEL that resulted in his poisoning, SENT ME CRAWLING
TO THE BATHROOM SHITTING LIKE A MINK, kind of makes me think
of the publishing luncheon scene in THE BELL JAR, crab salad in the centers
of AVOCADO PEARS, the discussion on constructing accessories
from mink tails and then it turns out the crab was bad, THE SICKNESS
ROLLED THROUGH ME IN GREAT WAVES. AFTER EACH WAVE
IT WOULD FADE AWAY AND LEAVE ME LIMP AS A WET LEAF
AND SHIVERING ALL OVER AND THEN I WOULD FEEL IT
RISING UP IN ME AGAIN, Bourdain said don't order fish on a Monday,
as it's likely left over from the weekend rush stock, best to wait
for what's fresh, though also he expressed the belief that it's wrong
to let delicacies, even when suspect, go untried, I HAVE NO WISH TO DIE,
he wrote, but still, IF YOU'RE WILLING TO RISK SOME SLIGHT
LOWER GI DISTRESS . . . FOR A SLICE OF PIZZA YOU JUST *KNOW*
HAS BEEN SITTING ON THE BOARD FOR AN HOUR OR TWO, WHY NOT
TAKE A CHANCE ON THE GOOD STUFF, and he mentioned, with admiration,
Rasputin, the reported routine of self-poisoning to accrue tolerance,
stave off attempts on his life, I've read in accounts of hunger
strikers that they sometimes come to consider their bodies as weapons,
THE ONLY WEAPON WE HAVE, when the doctor says SUPPOSE YOU TRY
AND TELL ME WHAT YOU THINK IS WRONG, the narrator of THE BELL JAR
tells us I TURNED THE WORDS OVER SUSPICIOUSLY, LIKE ROUND,
SEA-POLISHED PEBBLES THAT MIGHT SUDDENLY PUT OUT
A CLAW AND CHANGE INTO SOMETHING ELSE, that lunch just seems

so long ago, cold chicken and the PINK-MOTTLED CLAW MEAT
POKING SEDUCTIVELY THROUGH ITS BLANKET OF MAYONNAISE,
the YELLOW-GREEN of the AVOCADO PEAR, I EAT MEN LIKE AIR.

Suddenly

the cause they never
volunteered and we never asked and everyone
knew what that meant

what they said was SUDDENLY

making his end sound epiphanic, the apple
beaning Isaac Newton or keen Scheherazade attuning

to the stupefying force of narrative, THE ONLY
WEAPON WE HAVE

I've read stories

rich men in vindictive fervor, taking it out
on dogs and servants
the accrual of despair, the tyrant's whim

less sudden it couldn't
have been

Suffrutescent Scrub

as a child I was taken
with a story I'd read in some
volume about a traveler who'd died
in Death Valley not of heat

but of cold—determined to set
the world record for longest
exposure, he'd packed his body
in ice enough to do him in

I think of him any time
your name is mentioned or God
forbid we encounter each
other—I think of his terminal

overcompensation as I insist what
a gift you are, the gentlest gem
of this city, it's always so good
to see you it's so so good

I Tune My Body and My Brain to the Music of the Land

An important part of becoming any actor
is showing up to a room full of people who look
more or less like you, all auditioning for the same bit part.
I guess some find this threatening and/or a source
of destabilization, but, for me, my everyday activities
already leave me so threatened and destabilized
that it's hard to imagine a throng of look-alikes
making that much of a dent. Asked why he didn't paint

from nature, Jackson Pollock responded I AM NATURE.
Asked why I don't live in an admittedly flawed
utopian experiment in which work is substituted
for property as the basis of social belonging,
I say I AM AN ADMITTEDLY FLAWED UTOPIAN
EXPERIMENT IN WHICH WORK IS SUBSTITUTED
FOR PROPERTY AS THE BASIS OF SOCIAL
BELONGING. I spend all day reading magazine
columns and spitting back my own stories. My Most
Embarrassing Moment would have to be a tie

between when I forged NUMBER 1 (LAVENDER MIST)
using five separate pigments that weren't developed
until years after Pollock's death, and that time
I strutted through the neighborhood assuming
nobody but me could tell I was dead, when actually
half the street was texting each other SHE THINKS
WE DON'T NOTICE [eye-roll gif]. I want to be a better
person. Divest from bad habits. I also want to
just hop in the hedge and hide from it all, like the third
most surrendered domestic animals (rabbits).

My Teacher Again

I happened to meet, in a dream, my teacher again—at least
that's how I put it to friends, pretending as I often do
that the scene was not one of my conscious manufacture.
Really I'd just imagined it while entirely awake, while doing
something impossible for someone in the middle of sleeping,
snacking on carrots or needling a stuck bead
out from the floorboard crack. What my teacher wanted
so much to convey was that taking in a dog is for ego—
that people get off on being greeted after errands
as though they've returned from the sea. But what I love
about my dog is not her desperation for me, but how she does not
feel shame at her desperation, the way I feel shame
at my desperation for you, Ricky, each time you appear
in the sliver of kitchen at six in the morning, river of curls
untidy from sleeping. I've been up all night.

Quick Love Note

There are two types of people in this town:
astronomers, and those who want to fuck
astronomers, hoping to get stars christened
in their honor. Well, bad news:
most stars are named something like X8537—
nobody's honoring anything
except themselves and numbers. I never fell
for the romance of telescopes:
the universe's enormity, our corresponding
infinitessitude. When I think of discovery,
I only think of turnoffs: blue dye in the organs,
mice shot into orbit, innovations
stewing in beakers under surface-mounted
lights. The only honest thing about outer
space is the way it's depicted
in films: planets reduced to planes of flame
and garbage, with fern-appointed ships
for the rich to escape. Promise me
no posterity, nothing extractable, no record,
nothing fixed like an eye on the stock of the sky
and maybe—I said maybe—I'll look your way.

And Certainly Not Least

those years they made me want to die
so much that after I died I wanted
to die it was like that poem

IN KYOTO
HEARING THE CUCKOO
I LONG FOR KYOTO

nostalgia indignation chagrin
I failed to recognize death as itself
it was like that riddle

WHAT HAS FOUR
LETTERS AND SOMETIMES
HAS NINE

stop waiting for an answer
it's simply a statement it's simply
a fact and saying you

owe me literal hundreds of literal
thousands of literal
dollars is simply a statement too

Isolette

So they can put a man on the moon but they won't
make a way for a living adult to go back and elect
to have never existed. To save from being raped
the person who had the person who had the person
who had the person who had me, would I give up
my life? Yeah, I would. I mean who
                                        needs it:
the hospital by the highway, the isolette, flat sheet—

I would give it all up ever and backward to save you,
even though, let's face it, what did you do

for me? For my woolly moment, which to you
is the future? Did you force a new world in which
I would be protected? That's a no. But I'm not
petty. I am in fact an enemy of the fixation with things
being square, the check split down to the penny.
It's my pleasure. It's
                        my pleasure. It's my treat.

Remember My Decision for One Day

Oh sure, keep referring to oxygenation
of the planet as a service
the woods provide. Everyone
is a worker. I was so sorry to learn of the shuttering
of the premiere coffeehouse in East Hampton—
I'd been looking forward
to never going there, and now I'll never get
to never go. I'd read about how it had those big
garage windows that tilt in the summer
to facilitate an indoor–outdoor setting,
allowing patrons to fantasize that they aren't
actually there. That they aren't having a nice flat white
and listening in on their neighbors,
the pronouncements on fondant
and figs and the forest, should the spruce
be extinguished or permitted
to burn, is destruction necessary, is extinction
built into nature, aren't we all inherently
brutal, isn't the quest for constancy futile, isn't it
beautiful to be fired, isn't there peace
in every pause, doesn't getting gutted
set you free, isn't that actually good for the tree?

THESE PALM TREES ARE DRIVING ME CRAZY . . .

(Claude Monet)
(while traveling with Renoir in the Italian Riviera)

Individual Normal Hill

in the same way your friends are the family
you choose your death place
is the birthplace you choose Monet
in Giverny and Mark Rothko in New York City and me
at the winter employee mixer just
kidding I didn't die I only struggled
like a bug in an eighth inch of rain and then randomly
smacked my way out I couldn't
die I had too much to do I had to hold
all incoming calls I had to outdistance
at least some detractors I had to tune in
to watch ski jump every four winters I had to get away
from the snobs in my life
who would drown themselves only in the Seine
I had to cement and declare my principles
the Scioto the Ohio the Olentangy any of these
is good enough for me

Straight Sets

ok I never went to Paris but that's
ok I said I'll have Paris here
deejay play Romantic Accordion Music
deejay play whatever starts with a breathy UN DEUX TROIS
a lime falls off the counter
that's the French Open is it true
that tennis grunts were originally encouraged
to mask the specific sound
of the racket making contact
so as not to reveal to the opposing player
the type of spin on the ball
I'm like that with sobbing it's strategic
I'm obscuring the sound
of me plotting my revenge
don't s'il vous plaît pretend you can ignore
how close I was to breakthrough
how devastating quel dommage it was to be shut down
on the precipice of discovery
at the very brink of knowledge
powerless against the defunding of my longitudinal
study to finally and incontestably
determine whether being born is worth it
mon dieu I can't believe we'll never know

Really Raining

Every time I've seen the moon, I've thought it was the Earth and I'm
somewhere else gazing at it, gauging whether I'll make it
back someday. Every time I've seen the sun, I've thought it was the Earth-moon
burning and said goodbye. I've always made a point, every time
I've seen rain, of announcing IT'S REALLY RAINING, even if it's just
a spattering here, a spattering there. WOW, IT'S COMING DOWN. Who am I,
I've said, to say what it's like in the spray for somebody else,
and by SOMEBODY ELSE I mean of course that bug, smacked over
by an eighth inch of water, splayed and aeriform. When you're slight
enough to be ended by a single drop, a single drop's a storm.

Can Art Be Taught

WHEN I AM IN CALIFORNIA, I AM NOT IN THE WEST.
I AM WEST OF THE WEST.

(Theodore Roosevelt)

When I am on West California Avenue
in the most populous city in Ohio, I am not on West
California Avenue in the most populous city in Ohio. I am
west of West California Avenue
in the capital city of Ohio. I am reading a book
that says there is only one story: HAMLET.
THE LION KING is HAMLET. SPIDERMAN is HAMLET. Ok, so
was it HAMLET when the real estate
powers changed the name of our neighborhood
in the fastest-growing though not most densely populated
part of Ohio from NORTH CAMPUS to OLDE NORTH COLUMBUS,
on the theory that the word CAMPUS would repel investors?
Was it HAMLET when there was no parallel
projected loss from the name COLUMBUS? I'm not surprised
there's only one story; I'm just surprised it's HAMLET.
I would have guessed it was Studs Terkel's
WILL THE CIRCLE BE UNBROKEN, in which an emergency
physician explains that he has to say DEAD
to the families—he can't be soft and say GONE or WE LOST HIM—
only DEAD can get itself understood. Was it HAMLET
when you killed me? Was it HAMLET when you killed me DEAD?
Is it HAMLET now, as I make myself so clear?

No One Calls It That

I'm not so petty that I can't put personal
feelings aside and congratulate you
on killing me, on killing me so immensely
dead, more dead than I'd ever
been killed before, and in fact so
dead that I overshot
death and ricocheted right back to life—
hey, take a bow. And I'm not so

proud that I can't say sorry—sorry to you
that I'm not still dead, that I
didn't die forever like someone sloshing
in the cold ocean in her seven
pairs of stockings after the wrecking
of the ROYAL MAIL SHIP TITANIC—

Months At Once

Doctor, it hurts when I cough. SO DON'T COUGH. Doctor, it also
hurts when the world is coughing
me up as though I'm money with which it's fiercely reluctant
to part. SO DON'T GET COUGHED LIKE A BAD LITTLE DOLLAR
THAT'S LODGED IN THE WORLD'S ACCOUNT.
Doctor, they say the only way to secure,
in these times, an apartment is to put down
months at once. And they say there is no
Heaven anymore and that now, when you die, you have to shift backward
into some underpopulated
slice of the past. Doctor, dying to me
seems anticlimactic. I spend so much time as it is in the dirt
and the stench and the sear that I fear
it'll happen without me taking note. SO TAKE NOTE.
Doctor, I know, when you inform me I'm dying, you'll stand
so far away from me you'll be nearly in the nurses' lounge or practically
in the parking lot or essentially on an airplane tens
of thousands of feet above the Earth and IS THERE
A DOCTOR ON THIS PLANE will boom out
from the intercom and you'll flag the attendant, but only to ask
which cocktails can they do. Doctor, make it two.

Rough Stuff

Whether or not to inform the dead, I can't make
up my mind. I just know how I am with them: the same
as with the living. With all they're going through, how can
I foist on them my sorrows. What will they say,
behind my back, to each other: Christ—she's aware
of what we're grappling with here (being dead) and still
she arrives at the grave, she arrives at the moss-drenched
meaningful creek, going on and on, detailing
the latest, soliciting guidance—some people, they can't
think of anything. Anything but themselves.

Careful

The good news is I just found out that I have,
like a cat, nine lives. The bad news
is that this one's number nine. I have to be
careful. I have to stay home a lot. Lots of TV.
I like it when a single actor appears
across multiple shows. It suggests that so much
is survivable. Last week this guy
was a mid-level gangster getting brutally
clubbed and then launched off a bridge; this week
he's a prep school teacher, snacking in the lounge.
I'm happy for him. He really turned it around.

Overall, I need to stop moving. On viewing
an establishing shot of the Toronto skyline, I felt
relief that I had no idea which city it was.
Nothing against Toronto—it's just nice
to not have so much be familiar.
I'm considering religion, but only the ones
with many miracles still to come. I don't
want one where the miracles already
happened. I need to stay home more. More
TV. It can't be correct that just demons and me
have what was done to us on our bodies forever.

That Endless Skyway

Look, I'm not going to apologize for grasping
your hand in greeting and in that moment gaining access
to all your memories of your most profound
moments of shame. It's a superpower
I have from having died and then having survived
my own death—let's not make
a big deal. I do of course receive the intermittent
objection that IT'S NOT FAIR, but, look, what

is? Is it fair that 77% of the habitat of US coastal redwoods
is under private ownership? Is it fair that Woody Guthrie
had to find out about the death of his mom
by receiving in the mail a check for one dollar and fifty cents,
the remaining funds in her hospital canteen account?
Is it fair that I, after being left for dead, at last

knew how the snow felt, tracked inside and not mopped up,
melting, floored? Is it fair to the snow
that it no longer lays claim to the exclusive experience
of that feeling, the very last thing the snow once had to itself?
You don't hear the snow complaining.
You don't hear its hexagonal whine. There's no I WANT
TO FEEL NATALIE'S FEELINGS; IT'S ONLY
RIGHT IF SHE'S GONNA GET TO FEEL MINE—

First of December

God come on stop cutting me
out of your photos God stop dragging
the mouse around my shopworn
body like a chalk outline then clicking FILL
WITH BACKGROUND God I know

that times are tight I know you only
made one death per person I'm sorry
to have snagged more than my
share but surely you've heard about TO EACH
ACCORDING TO HIS NEED and I guess

I got what I needed God I'm sorry
to those who find with time
that there aren't deaths left for them to die
but God you're the one who stokes
demand then chokes up the supply

Sorry to Eat

and run, but I'm just in this enormous
rush to die so I can haunt you. I really have to get moving. I'm actually
quite behind. My error was assuming
I was already dead and so could begin straight away; I take
full blame. I thought I remembered being drawn up
and out of myself and into the cosmos, but in fact
I was thinking of the time my boss dropped her keys
down a grate and we had to call the city to retrieve them with a magnet.
It turns out about half the incidents I once believed
to be my own memories are really just things that happened
to those keys. I recall so much firsthand unlocking
and so few human scenes, such as scrubbing a cake pan or tendering
a letter or sitting in mourning for the melting
of the ice caps while also respecting their apparent decision
to concretize their interior pain through visible self-destruction.
Don't think I don't know what you're doing,
choosing this place—the most crowded planet—to give me
the brush-off, assuming I won't make a scene. Don't think I won't scream.

Have You Been Wanting to Go to Sleep and Not Wake Up

I answered no, having long contended
that sleep offers only the drawbacks
of death (inability to partake in nature and drugs)
without the big benefit (no longer
being alive). Sleeping forever:
no thanks. I have, though, been wanting to take up
acting, in order to get myself a death scene.
The key is the constructed landscape, going out
in front of a plywood backdrop: barbershop
or bed of rocks—it doesn't
matter. What matters is securing
a different world to die in, as I refuse
to die in this one. I won't give it
the satisfaction. Not that it is ever satisfied.

Notes

The untruncated quotation is as follows: I DON'T HAVE ANY SEINE RIVER LIKE MONET; I'VE JUST GOT U.S. 66 BETWEEN OKLAHOMA AND LOS ANGELES (Ed Ruscha).

An alternate version of this book began with the epigraph HELPLESS HELPLESS HELPLESS HELPLESS (Neil Young). A corresponding alternate version of this NOTES section began with the information that it's sort of hard to tell, from the way the lead and backing vocals overlap in the song from which this line is drawn, whether the line is most faithfully rendered on the page as HELPLESS HELPLESS HELPLESS or HELPLESS HELPLESS HELPLESS HELPLESS.

An alternate alternate version of this book began with the epigraph HELPLESS HELPLESS HELPLESS, with the corresponding alternate alternate version of the NOTES section beginning THE UNTRUNCATED QUOTATION IS AS FOLLOWS: HELPLESS HELPLESS HELPLESS HELPLESS.

AN AMERICAN IN PARIS, dir. Vincente Minnelli (1951).

Sanford Meisner's book SANFORD MEISNER ON ACTING begins with an epigraph from Goethe: I WISH THE STAGE WERE AS NARROW AS THE WIRE OF A TIGHTROPE DANCER, SO THAT NO INCOMPETENT WOULD DARE STEP UPON IT.

George Henry Lewes's ON ACTORS AND THE ART OF ACTING refers to the actor's task of displaying extreme emotion on cue as the need to STRIKE TWELVE AT ONCE. Lewes recounts the lore of the eighteenth-century Shakespearean actor William Macready, who was said to use his time backstage to work himself up INTO AN IMAGINATIVE RAGE BY CURSING SOTTO VOCE, AND SHAKING VIOLENTLY A LADDER FIXED AGAINST THE WALL.

Wow ok dude must be nice to have lived in circumstances where over-powering rage felt remote enough that you had to develop your whole ladder protocol to feel it.

Zukin, Sharon. LOFT LIVING: CULTURE AND CAPITAL IN URBAN CHANGE (1982).

Breslin, James E.B. MARK ROTHKO: A BIOGRAPHY (2012).

In April 1971, for his MFA thesis, Chris Burden confined himself for five straight days in Locker Number Five on the arts quad of the University of California, Irvine; this piece would go on to be widely considered a transformational moment in the history of performance art. Today, the locker remains on the campus, unmarked, in a second-floor outdoor corridor. The lock is owned by Gagosian.

I HAVE BUT ONE AMBITION FOR ALL MY PICTURES—THAT THEIR INTENSITY BE FELT UNEQUIVOCALLY AND IMMEDIATELY (Mark Rothko).

Hedda Sterne died in New York City in 2011 at the age of 100.

WHEN BEGGARS DIE THERE ARE NO COMETS SEEN;
THE HEAVENS THEMSELVES BLAZE FORTH THE DEATH OF PRINCES. (Calpurnia, JULIUS CAESAR, Act 2, Scene 2).

FARGO, dir. Joel & Ethan Coen (1996).

As is to be expected, there is no single consensus English translation of Blaise Cendrars's 1913 LA PROSE DU TRANSSIBÉRIEN ET DE LA PETITE JEHANNE DE FRANCE. The translation here is by John Dos Passos (1931).

When I first read the poem commonly referred to in English as THE PROSE OF THE TRANS-SIBERIAN, I got confused and thought the GREAT SCAFFOLD was the Eiffel Tower, but then I was like oh come on Nattie he *just* mentioned the Eiffel Tower like two words ago when he said THE ONLY TOWER.

The GREAT SCAFFOLD is the guillotine, obviously.

(GREAT SCAFFOLD translated alternately by Ron Padgett [1993] as GREAT GIBBET.)

The six principal pollutants, as articulated by the United States Environmental Protection Agency, are: carbon monoxide, lead, nitrogen oxide, ground-level ozone, particulates, sulfur oxide.

The FOUR JEWELS OF THE CELEBRITY ENDORSEMENT DOLLAR, as articulated in JERRY MAGUIRE (dir. Cameron Crowe [1996]) are: shoe, car, clothing line, soft drink.

Herman, Judith. TRAUMA AND RECOVERY: THE AFTERMATH OF VIO-LENCE—FROM DOMESTIC ABUSE TO POLITICAL TERROR (1992).

I USED TO DO DRUGS. I STILL DO, BUT I USED TO, TOO (Mitch Hedberg).

O TRUE APOTHECARY,
THY DRUGS ARE QUICK. THUS WITH A KISS I DIE. (Romeo, ROMEO AND JULIET, Act 5, Scene 3).

LOS ANGELES PLAYS ITSELF, dir. Thom Andersen (2003).

In INDEPENDENCE DAY (dir. Roland Emmerich [1996]), when Captain Steven Hiller, portrayed by Will Smith, encounters an extraterrestrial, he pulls the creature from its ship, punches it in the face, and says the three little words every true romantic longs to hear:

WELCOME TO EARTH.

On at least one occasion, I have written about hiking to the Hollywood sign and employed the word OBVERSE to refer to the sign's back side, even though OBVERSE means the front. I regret the error.

I AM HEARTILY ASHAMED OF THE THINGS I HAVE WRITTEN IN THE PAST (Mark Rothko).

PRETTY WOMAN, dir. Garry Marshall (1990). When Los Angeles sex worker Vivian Ward, portrayed by Julia Roberts, reenters the Rodeo Drive dress shop where she'd earlier been snubbed, she flaunts the extravagant purchases made at other stores and (depending on how you look at it), in either a long-deserved triumph of self-respect or a wanton display of class treason, inquires of the sales clerk: YOU WORK ON COMMISSION, RIGHT?

THAT'S NOT BLOOD—THAT'S RED (Jean-Luc Godard).

11 million metric tons of plastic are estimated to end up in the ocean each year. A person is estimated to consume an annual amount of plastic equivalent to one standard-size credit card.

YOU WORK ON COMMISSION, RIGHT?

The first time Rodin saw the ocean, he said IT IS A MONET.

In CLUELESS (dir. Amy Heckerling [1995]), Cher Horowitz, portrayed by Alicia Silverstone, derides another girl at a Los Angeles party as A FULL-ON MONET, meaning that the girl is OK at a distance but A BIG OLD MESS up close.

Legendary acting teacher Stella Adler said of her husband, director Harold Clurman: HE WAS A PUBLIC MAN. . . . HE HAD NO TALENT AS A PRIVATE MAN.

Ways of writing Mark Rothko's original name I have encountered include: Markus Rothkowitz, Marcus Rothkowicz, Ма́ркус Ротко́вич.

The untruncated quotation is as follows: TODAY HAMLET, TOMORROW A SUPERNUMERARY, BUT EVEN AS A SUPERNUMERARY YOU MUST BECOME AN ARTIST. This was the motto of the Moscow Art Theatre (est. 1898), which laid the foundations of what would come to be called method acting.

WHEN YOU TURNED YOUR BACK TO THE PAINTING, YOU WOULD FEEL THAT PRESENCE THE WAY YOU FEEL THE SUN ON YOUR BACK (Mark Rothko).

It is rare to encounter a biographical account of Claude Monet that doesn't mention his single unsuccessful suicide attempt, in 1868, in the Seine.

WELCOME TO EARTH.

Other facts about Monet include: Monet loved driving he had six cars that's true he also smoked a ton and charged his daughters with orbiting him while he painted so they could pick up the half-smoked cigarettes he'd thrown on the ground and place them in a bucket so he could smoke the other halves later wow Monet.

Plath, Sylvia. THE BELL JAR (1963).

Bourdain, Anthony. KITCHEN CONFIDENTIAL (2000).

Mallett, David. GARDEN SONG (1975).

WELCOME TO EARTH.

As is to be expected, there is no single consensus English translation of Matsuo Bashō's seventeenth-century haiku. The translation here is by Jane Hirshfield (2017).

Sometimes rendered alternately on chyrons as NORMAL INDIVIDUAL HILL.

Theodore Butler, the impressionist hired by the United States military to paint eight large landscapes for trainees to practice firing on, also died in Giverny. Rodin died in Meudon. Anthony Bourdain died in Kaysersberg-Vignoble. Gene Kelly, who portrayed a painter and former soldier living in France in the 1951 film AN AMERICAN IN PARIS, and who spoke on film the line BROTHER, IF YOU CAN'T PAINT IN PARIS,

YOU'D BETTER GIVE UP AND MARRY THE BOSS'S DAUGHTER, died in Beverly Hills.

I HAVE PAINTED THE SEINE THROUGHOUT MY LIFE, AT EVERY HOUR, AT EVERY SEASON. I HAVE NEVER TIRED OF IT: FOR ME THE SEINE IS ALWAYS NEW (Claude Monet).

Acknowledgments

Thank you to Becky Alexander, Rachel Applebaum, Brandy Barents, Kevin Barents, Stephanie Burt, Roxi Carter, Adam Clay, Lee Edelman, Big Egg, Sorelle Friedler, Sarah Gilbert, Kevin H., Erika Hansen, Matt Hooley, Kerry Howley, Jane Hu, Laurel Kean, Josh Kotin, Jess Lacher, Tanya Larkin, Andrew Lehman, Sandra Lim, Joe Litvak, Lisa Lowe, Jake Marmer, Ted Martin, Annie McClanahan, Tyler Meier, Anahid Nersessian, Shoshana Olidort, Barry Shank, Shari Speer, Lindsay Turner, Annie Wagner, Jennifer Wehunt, Jillian Weise, and Nate Wolff.

Thank you to Kathy Fagan Grandinetti and Pablo Tanguay, first readers of many of the poems here.

Thank you to Rebecca Morgan Frank and Meg Shevenock for conversations that carried this project through.

Thank you to the Department of English and the School of Humanities at the University of California, Irvine. Thank you to the UCI Programs in Writing and to Michelle Latiolais, Claire Vaye Watkins, and Monica Youn. Gratitude and admiration to all my students for their deep thinking and writing. This book was completed with the invaluable assistance of a residency fellowship from the Studios at MASS MoCA.

Thank you to Michael Wiegers and everyone at Copper Canyon Press. Thank you to Anthony Anaxagorou and everyone at Out-Spoken Press, which first published some of these poems in the pamphlet *Today Hamlet*. Thank you to the editors and staff of the magazines and journals in which others of these poems were first published, sometimes in alternative versions: *The American Poetry Review, And Other Poems, At What Cost, Autocorrect, Basket, Bennington Review, The Drift, Granta, The Hopkins Review, Iterant, The London Review of Books, The New Yorker,*

The New York Review of Books, Northwest Review, Poetry, Poetry Northwest, The Poetry Review, The Rumpus, Southern Indiana Review, Sugar House Review, Washington Square Review.

Thank you to Martha.

Thank you to all my parents and to my in-laws, to my sister and my siblings-in-law and my nephew.

Thank you to Ricky and Frances.

Frances, when you are young, I assume you know all things—

About the Author

Natalie Shapero's writing has appeared in *The New Yorker, The New York Times Magazine, The London Review of Books, The Paris Review, The Nation,* and other journals. She is the author of the poetry collections *Popular Longing* (2021), *Hard Child* (2017), and *No Object* (2013), and she has performed at the Pulitzer Arts Foundation, the Poetry Project at St. Marks, and elsewhere. She lives in Los Angeles and teaches writing at UC Irvine.

POETS FOR POETRY

Copper Canyon Press poets are at the center of all our efforts as a nonprofit publisher. Poets create the art of our books, and they read and teach the books we publish. Many are also generous donors who believe in financially supporting the vibrant poetry community of Copper Canyon Press. For decades, our poets have quietly donated their royalties, have contributed their time to our fundraising campaigns, and have made personal donations in support of emerging and established poets. Their generosity has encouraged the innovative risk-taking that sustains and furthers the art form.

The donor-poets who have contributed to the Press since 2023 include:

Jonathan Aaron

Pamela Alexander

Kazim Ali

Ellen Bass

Erin Belieu

Mark Bibbins

Linda Bierds

Sherwin Bitsui

Jaswinder Bolina

Marianne Boruch

Laure-Anne Bosselaar

Cyrus Cassells

Peter Cole and Adina Hoffman

Elizabeth J. Coleman

Shangyang Fang

John Freeman

Forrest Gander

Jenny George

Dan Gerber

Jorie Graham

Roger Greenwald

Robert and Carolyn Hedin

Bob Hicok

Ha Jin

The estate of Jaan Kaplinski

Laura Kasischke

Jennifer L. Knox

Ted Kooser

Stephen Kuusisto

Deborah Landau

Sung-Il Lee

Ben Lerner

Dana Levin

Maurice Manning

Heather McHugh

Jane Miller

Roger Mitchell

Lisa Olstein

Gregory Orr

Eric Pankey

Kevin Prufer

Alicia Rabins

Dean Rader

Paisley Rekdal

James Richardson

Alberto Ríos

David Romtvedt

Sarah Ruhl

Kelli Russell Agodon

Natalie Shapero

Arthur Sze

Yuki Tanaka

Elaine Terranova

Chase Twichell

Ocean Vuong

Connie Wanek

Emily Warn

Poetry is vital to language and living. Since 1972, Copper Canyon Press has published extraordinary poetry from around the world to engage the imaginations and intellects of readers, writers, booksellers, librarians, teachers, students, and donors.

WE ARE GRATEFUL FOR THE MAJOR SUPPORT PROVIDED BY:

ARTSFUND

THE PAUL G. ALLEN
FAMILY FOUNDATION

Hawthornden
Foundation

INGRAM
CONTENT GROUP

McSWEENEY'S

WASHINGTON STATE
ARTS COMMISSION

 ART WORKS. | National Endowment for the Arts arts.gov

The Witter Bynner Foundation
for Poetry

TO LEARN MORE ABOUT UNDERWRITING
COPPER CANYON PRESS TITLES,
PLEASE CALL 360-385-4925 EXT. 105

WE ARE GRATEFUL FOR THE MAJOR SUPPORT PROVIDED BY:

Anonymous

Jill Baker and Jeffrey Bishop

Anne and Geoffrey Barker

Mona Baroudi and Patrick
   Whitgrove

Lisha Bian

John Branch

Diana Broze

John R. Cahill

Sarah J. Cavanaugh

Keith Cowan and Linda Walsh

Peter Currie

Geralyn White Dreyfous

The Evans Family

Mimi Gardner Gates

Claire Gribbin

Gull Industries Inc.
   on behalf of William True

Carolyn and Robert Hedin

David and Jane Hibbard

Bruce S. Kahn

Phil Kovacevich and Eric Wechsler

Eric La Brecque

Maureen Lee and Mark Busto

Ellie Mathews and Carl Youngmann
   as The North Press

Kathryn O'Driscoll

Petunia Charitable Fund and
   advisor Elizabeth Hebert

Suzanne Rapp and Mark Hamilton

Adam and Lynn Rauch

Emily and Dan Raymond

Joseph C. Roberts

Cynthia Sears

Kim and Jeff Seely

Tree Swenson

Julia Sze

Donna Wolf

Jamie Wolf

Barbara and Charles Wright

In honor of C.D. Wright
   from Forrest Gander

Caleb Young as C. Young Creative

The dedicated interns and faithful
   volunteers of Copper Canyon Press

The pressmark for Copper Canyon Press
suggests entrance, connection, and interaction
while holding at its center
an attentive, dynamic space for poetry.

This book is set in Adobe Garamond Pro.
Book design by Gopa & Ted2, Inc.
Printed on archival-quality paper.